CROWNED HEART SERIES – BOOK FIVE

Dorothy Baker

Written by Melanie Lotfali
Illustrated by Era Frost

The Crowned Heart series – Dorothy Baker

Written by Melanie Lotfali
Illustrated by Era Frost

Copyright © National Spiritual Assembly
of the Bahá'ís of Australia Inc. All Rights Reserved

Bahá'í Publications Australia
Softcover ISBN 978-1-923266-13-1
Hardcover ISBN 978-1-923266-14-8

Distributed by Bahá'í Distribution Services
173 Mona Vale Rd, Ingleside NSW 2101
bds@bahai.org.au
www.bahaibooks.com.au

Typeset using Sauna Pro

How many queens of the world have laid down their heads on a pillow of dust and disappeared... Not so the handmaids who ministered at the Threshold of God; these have shone forth like glittering stars in the skies of ancient glory, shedding their splendors across all the reaches of time.

‘Abdu'l-Bahá

There are queens who wear crowns on their heads. Their crowns are made of earthly things like gold and diamonds and rubies.

And there are queens who wear crowns in their hearts. Their crowns are made of heavenly things, like love and courage and humility. This is the story about one of those queens. Her name is Dorothy Baker.

Dorothy Baker met 'Abdu'l-Bahá when she was fourteen years old. 'Abdu'l-Bahá had come from the Holy Land to America to visit the Bahá'ís. After Dorothy met 'Abdu'l-Bahá, she wrote Him a letter begging Him to let her serve the Cause.

A few years later Dorothy was at the Bahá'í Temple and a thought came into her head that made her very worried. She thought, "What if I live my whole life without sacrificing for the Cause of God? What a waste my life will be! I will be like a tree with no fruit."

She started to cry and pray and cry and pray! She begged 'Abdu'l-Bahá to open the way for her to serve the the Cause with her whole heart. And of course, 'Abdu'l-Bahá heard her prayer and answered it.

Soon after that, Dorothy's grandmother – Mother Beecher – came to live with Dorothy. With Mother Beecher's help Dorothy developed the habit of studying the Writings for an hour or more each day. Sometimes she would say the Tablet of Ahmad every day for 19 days too. The Word of God was like water that cleaned the dirt from Dorothy's heart.

The mirror of Dorothy's heart became very shiny. It reflected the light of Bahá'u'lláh and Dorothy was able to teach many people about Him.

Soon Dorothy was studying and praying all day and teaching all night! People loved to hear Dorothy talk about the Bahá'í Teachings.

One day Dorothy gave a wonderful talk and everyone loved it. Dorothy was very pleased. But her dear friend, Louis Gregory gave her a warning. He told her to remember that she is like a flute that God is using to play beautiful music. He told her that if she gets proud, and forgets to be humble, the flute of her soul will get clogged up and no more music will come out.

Dorothy paid attention to the warning and begged 'Abdu'l-Bahá to keep her humble. Once again He answered her prayers. Dorothy became a wonderful Bahá'í speaker. She travelled all over the world telling people about Bahá'u'lláh.

One day Shoghi Effendi asked Dorothy to go to India for one month. She said, "Of course beloved Guardian!" Then he asked her to stay another month. She said, "Of course beloved Guardian!" And then another month! She was very tired but she said, "Of course beloved Guardian!"

Dorothy used every last bit of energy to tell people about the Bahá'í Faith. Finally after three months away, Dorothy got on a plane to go home. But instead of flying home, she flew to the Abhá Kingdom because her plane suddenly crashed!

Dorothy was a pure channel for God's love and Teachings to flow to the world, right up to the last minute of her life. The gem of humility shone brightly in the crown of Dorothy Baker's heart.

Hand of the Cause of God
Dorothy Baker

References

The stories and facts contained in this book are from:
  Barron Harper, *Lights of Fortitude*, August, 1997, George Ronald Publisher.
Dorothy Baker image © National Spiritual Assembly of the Bahá'ís of the United States.

Melanie Lotfali PhD is a graduate of the Australian College of Journalism in Professional Writing for Children. She is the author of the Fellowship Farm series, Unity in Diversity series, and Crowned Heart series.

Era Frost is a citizen of Earth. Through her stories and illustrations, she sends a message of love to all children in the world. She has been writing and illustrating stories since she was young and has worked as a book illustrator and designer since 2019. She has studied a Children's Publishing MA at Bath Spa University.

www.ingramcontent.com/pod-product-compliance
Lightning Source LLC
Chambersburg PA
CBHW041637040426
42449CB00021B/3490